WAR!

WAR!

Through the Eyes of a Child

DINAH DAY

iUniverse

WAR!
THROUGH THE EYES OF A CHILD

Copyright © 2014 Dinah Day.

All rights reserved. No part of this book may be used or reproduced by any means, graphic, electronic, or mechanical, including photocopying, recording, taping or by any information storage retrieval system without the written permission of the publisher except in the case of brief quotations embodied in critical articles and reviews.

iUniverse books may be ordered through booksellers or by contacting:

iUniverse
1663 Liberty Drive
Bloomington, IN 47403
www.iuniverse.com
1-800-Authors (1-800-288-4677)

Because of the dynamic nature of the Internet, any web addresses or links contained in this book may have changed since publication and may no longer be valid. The views expressed in this work are solely those of the author and do not necessarily reflect the views of the publisher, and the publisher hereby disclaims any responsibility for them.

Any people depicted in stock imagery provided by Thinkstock are models,
and such images are being used for illustrative purposes only.
Certain stock imagery © Thinkstock.

ISBN: 978-1-4917-4213-6 (sc)
ISBN: 978-1-4917-4214-3 (e)

Printed in the United States of America.

iUniverse rev. date: 10/21/2014

Baby Picture of Dinah Day

3 months old

CONTENTS

PART ONE: My Ancestral Roots
Sir Joshua Reynolds
My mother, Jane Moody Day (nee Husband)
My Grandmother, Dinah Elizabeth Husband (nee Reynolds)
My Great Grandmother with the crinoline dress
My father, Anthony Stanley Day
My sister, Emma Reynolds Day
My name is Dinah Elizabeth Morrison (nee Day)
Dr. Mearns

PART TWO: My Living Accommodation
Three-storey flat

PART THREE: The Innocence of Childhood
Bay of Nigg

PART FOUR: School Days
First day of school
My teacher, Miss Shaw
My teacher, Miss Fyfe
Disciplinary action, left hand to right hand
"Good morning, Miss Fyfe"
Dress code

PART FIVE: In Respect of my Dear Father
My Father was a fisherman in the North Sea.
The smell of tar
The depression and people on the dole

PART SIX: Childhood Games
One, two three O'Leary
Keiller's Jam

PART SEVEN: Church Activities
Dressed in our Sunday best clothes
Collection, "Hear the pennies dropping."
Walk in the park
Teatime

PART EIGHT: Childhood Illness
Toothache
Scarlet fever

PART NINE: Father's Ulcer
Special light foods

PART TEN: Emma and her Puppy, 'Beauty'
Dressed her up in baby clothes
Blew in face, bit my lip

PART ELEVEN: My Brother's Pets
Canary and pet mouse

PART TWELVE: Visits with Ma's Friends
Children should be seen and not heard.
Visiting friends in Belmedie
"It's okay, chicken."

PART THIRTEEN: My Seventh Birthday Party
Friends and music

PART FOURTEEN: Christmas
Special time of the year
Sunday school Christmas party
Pantomines

PART FIFTEEN: Holiday Hi-lights
Timber Market
Guy Fawkes Day
Hogmanay

PART SIXTEEN: Climate
Three months of winter

PART SEVENTEEN: The Change from Gas Light to Electric Light
A shilling to turn on electric meter

PART EIGHTEEN: The Lamplighter
Lit the lamps about 4:30 p.m.

PART NINETEEN: Farmers Market
Every Friday

PART TWENTY: Street Vendors
Selling fish from the cart, "Fresh fish, fresh fish!"
Selling vegetables from the cart, "Tatties, tatties, tatties (potatoes)"

PART TWENTY-ONE: War Years
Britain at war with Germany
"Don't cry Ma, I promise I will be good!"
Gas masks given out to everyone
Underground shelters
A big explosion
Ladies Work Party
Army barracks at the Bay of Niggs

PART TWENTY-TWO: Conclusion
My life from birth to a teenager
A great childhood in spite of the war
Loving parents
One cannot ask for more
Tears and joys

War!

MY ANCESTRAL ROOTS

As I look back on the Reynolds' side of my Family Tree, my ancestral relative, Sir Joshua Reynolds, born at Plympton, Devon, England on July 16th, 1723 and died 1792, was one of the most dominant figures in the history of British art.

This is as far back as I can go and so I will continue from there. Most of the information in this book was given to me by my Mother, Jane Moody. My Grandmother was Dinah Elizabeth Reynolds after whom I was named. Then there was my Great Grandmother, the elegant lady wearing the crinoline dress! I have no information regarding my Father's side of the family; only my own memories of my dearest Father.

I was born on the 17th day of July, 1928 at approximately 11 a.m. at 7 Glenbervie Road, Torry, Aberdeen, Scotland.

My Mother's name was Jane Moody Day. My Father's name was Anthony Stanley Day. My Sister's name was Emma Reynolds Day. My Brother's name was Stanley Day and my name is Dinah Elizabeth Day.

Now the life of Dinah Elizabeth Day begins.

Dr. Mearns was our family Doctor. I was about to be born. My sister, Emma, was sitting on the doorstep of our home when Dr. Mearns arrived, "Well, Emma", he said, "you will soon be a sister. I will let you know when the baby arrives. Just stay here."

MY LIVING ACCOMMODATION

We lived in a three-storey flat. The Doctor walked up the

stairs. We lived on the third floor. I was about to enter into the world. The flat we lived in consisted of two rooms, a living room and kitchen combined, one bedroom, a coal fireplace in the kitchen, a sink where all the washing up was done and a small pantry to store our provisions. Our fireplace was used for cooking and a gas oven was next to the fireplace. There was a recess in the living room in which my parents slept. In the kitchen, was a wooden table with four matching chairs, a sideboard in which to put our clothes and dishes, etc. I remember we had gas fixtures on the wall at either side of the fireplace. These were our only means of light. The toilet was on the landing and was shared with the other tenant. There was no bathtub.

The laundry facilities were in a separate building outside in the backyard. There was a wringer washing device, a boiler where we would heat the water and two wash tubs. Each tenant had a specific day for washing. There was a clothesline in the backyard where we would hang our clothes to dry. The wash would take a full day. Ironing was done the next day. We even starched the men's shirt collars. This is what I remember about our washing day.

THE INNOCENCE OF CHILDHOOD

I will now go back as far as I can remember. I was four years old when I wandered away from home. How I got to the Bay of Nigg near the breakwater, I will never know. I remember, I was playing near the rocks turning over small stones looking for crabs. While being with a boy the same age as me, I had no idea I was lost and everyone was looking for us. As a child, there was no fear. I can imagine the joy in my Mother's heart when she found me!

SCHOOL DAYS

I remember the first day of school. There was a huge blackboard on which the teacher would print the times tables and the students would chant, "one times one is one, one times two is two" and so on until we were finished the first lesson. My teacher's name was Miss Shaw. I liked her very much. She was a kind teacher.

Later on, when I was about seven years old, I had another teacher, Miss Fyfe. She was a very strict teacher. I can remember being told that I must not write with my left hand. We had inkwells at the top right-hand corner of our desks. We had to write with a pen. We would dip our pens in the inkwells and so the lessons began. Many times, I would get a large cane over my knuckles reminding me that I must not write with my left hand. I remember being very nervous. I found it difficult to write with my right hand. My teacher won the battle over my penmanship but that was the only battle she won. I did everything else with my left hand.

At 9 a.m., the teacher rang a large brass bell reminding us that school was about to begin. We lined up to go into our classrooms. We were very respectful towards our teachers. We were taught to say as we all stood up, "Good Morning Miss Fyfe" and so on and so on. We always said the Lord's Prayer before the lessons began.

The dress code was a navy blue gym tunic with a white blouse, navy blue knickers with a pocket at the side for a handkerchief, a white undershirt (simmet, which we called it in our days), navy blue three-quarter stockings and black shoes. We wore a navy blue blazer and carried a leather school bag in which we kept our schoolbooks.

Lunch was from 12 noon to 1 p.m.. We had two breaks,

one in the morning and one in the afternoon. At 4 p.m., school ended for the day.

IN RESPECT OF MY DEAR FATHER

My Father was a fisherman. He trawled in the North Sea. The trawler he was in was manned by ten members including himself. He was a hardworking man. He was at Sea for ten days at a time. He was out in all kinds of weather.

Many times, when the wind howled, I awakened in the middle of the night from a deep sleep. I was scared of the wind, mostly because I heard my Mother saying, "Your poor Father is out there 'blashing' his face at sea." Blashing meant 'facing the storm'. These words haunt me still to this day.

I looked forward to the day when my Father came home. I peered out of the kitchen window and when I saw him come up the brae (a small hill), I jumped down the stairs, two at a time, and met him coming up the brae. He lifted me up in his arms. What a happy time that was for me. I still remember the joy in my heart to this day.

My Father carried a duffle bag over his shoulder. Inside the duffle bag were all his work clothes. He carried another brown woven bag full of fresh fish that he had caught at Sea. The fresh fish were shared amongst the people on the brae.

My Mother sent me with fresh fish to the neighbours. She told me, "Dinah, don't take anything if it is offered to you." Suffice to say, each neighbour who received fish gave me a penny. In turn, I replied, "Ma said I can't take anything." Of course, I was made to take the penny! I told my mother what was given to me and, in turn, she said, "That's alright, as long as you didn't ask for it." I was allowed to keep the pennies and spent them on sweeties (candies). I shared the sweeties with my friends. Everyone was happy.

My Father had a smell of tar about him, probably because of the fishing nets. Whatever it was, I loved that smell. It was my Da!

I dreaded the day when he had to leave. Three days went too fast. I remember seeing my Ma kissing my Da good-bye. I looked up to my Da's face and asked for my kiss. I remember sitting on my Da's knee. I always felt safe and secure when he was home. My Da made me the happiest girl in the whole world.

Ma was a good mother. She didn't have much money and what she had wasn't really enough on which to live.

Da didn't have a good income in my day. The fishermen were very poorly paid. The depression hit everyone. People were out of work. They lined up for jobs only to be turned down. People were on the 'dole' (in other words, unemployed).

As a child, we didn't understand. We had no idea what it was like for our parents. We didn't have much to eat. I remember having homemade soup made from a marrowbone, carrots and turnip and lentils. After the soup, we had 'mince and tatties' (potatoes and peas). We were glad to get anything and never complained because 'that was how it was'.

Teatime was at 5 p.m.. We usually had fish and chips or an egg.

CHILDHOOD GAMES

As children, we played games. Skipping was the girls' favourite game. Boys played with marbles or a spinning top. We all played ball. While bouncing the ball, we chanted all kinds of rhymes like this one.

Dinah Day

> *One, two, three O'Leary,*
> *I spy Mrs. Peerie,*
> *Sitting on her bumble eerie,*
> *Eating chocolate sweeties.*

I don't know what it means to this day but that's what we chanted. Here is another rhyme we chanted.

> *Keiller's Jam, Keiller's Jam,*
> *I love Keiller's Jam,*
> *My mother said to me,*
> *"What would you like for tea?"*
> *I looked upon the table.*
> *I saw butter, bread and jam*
> *but the only jam that I liked*
> *was Keiller's Jam!*

Strange how we remember all these sayings after so many years.

CHURCH ACTIVITIES

Church was a great part of our lives. Mother saw to that! We always got dressed in our Sunday best clothes. We never wore them any other time, just Sunday. Mother and I went to Church at 11 am. I sat beside her. Mother's famous words were, "NOW BE GOOD." How could I be bad in Church? I would fidget with my feet, look bored, then ask my Mother, giving her a nudge in the ribs, "Am I good?" She would say, "Sh-h-h!" That was all she said. I found the Church service very boring, I wondered if the Minister would ever stop talking. Oh, for the last hymn, hallelujah!

I loved Sunday school. That was more for me. The minister's wife would tell us lovely stories about Jesus and how he loved children. She was a lovely lady. She also had a box of candies. She handed one candy to each of us. She took up a collection. We put our pennies in a brass box as it was passed around to each of us. We sang this song.

Hear the pennies dropping,
Listen while they fall,
Everyone for Jesus,
He shall have them all.
Dropping, dropping, dropping, dropping,
Hear the pennies fall,
Everyone for Jesus,
He shall have them all.

Sunday was a special day. We always had a Sunday dinner. We usually had roast beef, potatoes and Yorkshire pudding, ice-cream and pineapple chunks.

After dinner, we went for a walk in the park. That was the thing in my day. We were never allowed to play outside on Sunday. That was a 'No No'.

Teatime on Sunday was sandwiches and small cupcakes and in the evening, before going to bed, we had cocoa made with water, milk and sugar.

CHILDHOOD ILLNESS

I remember having a toothache and wakening up during the night crying with pain. Ma gave me cloves to dull the pain. They never worked. I thought the night would never come to an end. The next day, she took me to a dentist. The tooth had to come out. The dentist gave me 'gas'. He asked me to bite down on something. Then, he put a mask over my mouth. Suddenly, everything was going 'round and round'. When I came to, I remember being sick to my stomach. I never ever *liked dentists.*

I remember having Scarlet Fever. I was in the hospital for some time. I remember Ma coming to see me. She looked through the window. She wasn't allowed into the ward. I remember being scared.

FATHER'S ULCER

I remember my Father being rushed home from Sea. He had a busted ulcer in his stomach. He was very sick. I remember Ma having to give him special light foods.

EMMA AND HER PUPPY, 'BEAUTY'

My sister Emma was eight years and four months older than me. She was working when I was nine years old. She worked for a man called Mr. James who ran a grocery store in town. He gave a dog to my sister. It was a Yorkshire Terrier. When she brought the puppy home, it was the cutest little dog I had ever seen. Emma named her puppy, 'Beauty'. I had so much fun with Beauty. I dressed her up in baby clothes and put glasses on to her. She let me do anything I wanted. She slept at the bottom of our bed. Emma and I slept in the same bed.

We moved to another flat, number 9 Glenbervie Road with three rooms. Now, my Brother, Stanley, had his own room.

Like I was saying, I had so much fun with Beauty. One day, when I was playing with Beauty, I blew into her face and she shook her head with a funny expression. I started to laugh and blew into her face again. Beauty did not think this was the least bit funny. She turned on me and bit my lip. Mother was scared after that happened. Seemingly, Beauty had bitten other people unknown to any of us. Mother took her to the vet. We couldn't keep her with us any longer in case she bit someone else. I was so unhappy afterwards. Emma wouldn't talk to my Mother. Emma blamed me for what happened. That was one of the saddest days of my life.

MY BROTHER'S PETS

My brother, Stanley, caught a canary on the Chain Bridge at the river Dee. Mother managed to get a cage for the canary. It was a prize bird. No one had claimed the canary so Stanley became the owner. We had the canary for quite a long time. One day, when I came home from school, I thought I would give the canary a drink of water. I put my hand into the cage to give it a drink and the next thing I knew, it went limp in my hand. I sat it up on the perch but it didn't move. It just fell over. I was panic-stricken.

'Whatever happened to the canary?'

I will never forget what happened to the canary as long as I live. The canary's death was a tragedy in my young life.

'What did I know about death?'

My brother asked me what I did to the canary. How did I know? One minute I was giving him a drink and then he went limp. We all shed tears that day.

My brother had a pet mouse. It was kept in a cage. It was the cutest little white mouse. My brother bought a quarter of a pound of cheese for the mouse and put it into the cage. The next morning, the cheese was gone and the mouse had gone to 'Mouse-Heaven'. It must have overeaten itself.

We certainly had some unhappy moments with our loving

pets but that's life.

VISITS WITH MA'S FRIENDS

We were well disciplined by Mother. She would not tolerate any 'talking back'.

I remember another incident when I about ten years old. Mother took me to visit her friends for afternoon tea. She told me not to ask for anything unless it was offered. We all sat around the table that displayed lots of fancy cakes. I spied one I liked. Being as I was not to ask for it, I said nothing until I saw a hand go to the fancy cake that I had been eyeing. Immediately, I started to cry. The lady of the house said, "What's the matter, dear?" I said, "She took my cake." My Mother stared at me with 'daggers' in her eyes. "Wait until you get home young lady. You're going to get a good lickin' for asking."

I remember one time Mother was going to visit some friends out of town. It was a small country village called Belmedie, not too far away maybe about eight miles. I promised I would cycle out to Belmedie to meet her. Well, in the meantime, my friends were going in another direction. I thought I could cycle with my friends, at first, and make it to Belmedie, on time. Needless to say, I didn't go to Belmedie but went with my friends, instead. My Mother was furious with me. She told me everyone was looking for me. She thought I had been in an accident. Well, I never heard the end of that experience. She was going to take my bicycle back to the store. It was a second-hand bicycle but it was mine. I got a good lickin' that night. My Father was home that day, and he must have felt sorry for me. He came into my room. I was sobbing myself to sleep. He said, "It's okay, chicken (his pet name for me). I will see that she doesn't take away your bike." I felt much better.

MY SEVENTH BIRTHDAY PARTY

I remember my seventh birthday and a delicious cake with lots of whipping cream and icing. I had a few friends over. Some of my friends gave me ankle socks and some gave me handkerchiefs. I loved that party.

Mother put a record on the gramophone. It was one of those old-fashioned gramophones with a handle that had to be cranked to make it work. She played the same record all the time. It was called 'Tip Toe Through the Tulips'.

CHRISTMAS

Christmas was a special time of the year. We hung our stockings on the mantelpiece and hoped we would find something in them. We usually got an orange and an apple and a few sweeties.

We attended Church for the Christmas Eve midnight service. That was our Christmas. We didn't get toys from our parents, just a stocking filled with fruits and sweeties.

I remember the Sunday school Christmas party that was held in the Church hall. There was always a Christmas tree beautifully decorated on the stage. All the hall lights were dimmed. Santa knocked very loudly on the door and made his entrance. There was so much excitement that night. Santa went up on the stage and gave each one of us a Christmas present. The boys got a truck or a book and the girls got a doll or a sewing kit. Everyone received a present. Our Church Christmas party was a great time for all of us children.

I remember the pantomimes leading up to Christmas. We

rehearsed for three months and the pantomimes were shown for three nights. I remember I was a Fairy Queen. It wasn't a big part because I was one of the young ones.

HOLIDAY HI-LIGHTS

TIMBER MARKET: We had different holidays. One stands out in my mind. It was called 'Timber Market' when we would go to town with our parents. It was a kind of market where there were wooden toys for sale. It was a great day! There were all kinds of candies. We sang this song.

*Today is Timber Market,
We're all dressed in blue.
Blue ribbons in our hair,
Sweeties in our moo. (mouth)*

I still don't know why we sang this song; 'we just did'.

GUY FAWKES DAY: 'Guy Fawkes Day' was another special day. We celebrated this day on the 5th of November. In 1605, Guy Fawkes, an English conspirator famous for his part in the 'Gunpowder Plot' was a member of a prominent Yorkshire family. His early religious training was in the Anglican faith but after his Father's death in 1579 and his Mother's subsequent marriage to a Roman Catholic, he was converted to Roman Catholicism.

His religious zeal, as well as his adventurous spirit, led him to leave England in 1593 and enlist in the Spanish Army in the Netherlands where he won a reputation for great courage and cool determination. He remained with the Spanish Army until April, 1604.

Meanwhile in England, a small group of disgruntled Catholics, lead by Robert Catesby, was forming plans to blow up the Parliament building where the King and his chief ministers were present. Since the plotters were well known and easily recognizable, they needed the assistance of a person with military experience who had been away from England for some time. The plotters decided upon Fawkes and early in April, 1604, Catesby sent his cousin, Thomas Winter, to the Netherlands to enlist Fawkes' services. Without being informed of the details of the plot, Fawkes returned to England and was soon brought into the conspiracy.

He took the name, John Johnson, and posed as a servant when the plotters rented a house abutting upon the Parliament building. Fawkes, disguised as a porter, stood sentinel while the other conspirators attempted to dig a subterranean passage to a point directly under the chamber of the House of Lords. When this project was abandoned and the conspirators rented an adjoining cellar, which extended under the Parliament building, Fawkes was given the task of planting the explosives. He brought in at least twenty barrels of gunpowder, placed several bars upon them to increase the impact of the explosion and then concealed these instruments of destruction with a covering of faggots and coals.

The gunpowder was, of course, never exploded. The Government learned of the plot before parliament met and Fawkes was arrested on the evening of November 4th, 1605. At first, he refused to name his fellow conspirators but after being tortured on the rack, he revealed all. He was tried before a special commission on January 27th, 1606 and was found guilty and was executed opposite the Parliament building four days later.

The scheduled date of the plot, November 5th, Guy Fawkes Day is celebrated in England with fireworks and the burning of 'guys'.

We, as children, made an effigy of Guy Fawkes and

burned it in a huge bonfire with fireworks. That was one of the special nights when we were allowed out late at night.

These are the words we chanted.

> Remember, remember,
> The fifth of November,
> The Gunpowder Plot in the hall.

HOGMANAY: Hogmanay, another celebration, was on December 31. The festivities lasted until the wee hours of the morning. Everything in the house had to be cleaned. Hogmanay was supposed to bring good luck. The table was set with all kinds of cakes, wines and whisky.

The most important person had to be a dark-haired man. He would knock at the door at 12 midnight, not a minute before. He usually had a bottle of whisky with him and poured a drink for each person. The children were only given a fruit drink or ginger beer.

Hogmanay started off the New Year's celebrations. New Year's Day was a holiday for everyone. We were happy! We sang all the old Scottish songs, danced and were merry.

As a child, I enjoyed watching the older people having a good time. Hogmanay was the one and only night of the year when we were allowed to stay up until after midnight.

CLIMATE

The winter in Scotland lasted about three months from December until the end of February.

There was a big hill across the road from where I lived. We sledged down the hill. There was no traffic so we had a *great time.*

I remember when I went into the house after sledging. My face was rosy red. My fingers and toes tingled from the cold. Mother put my clothes near the fire to dry. We had no electric dryers in my day so we depended on the fire to dry our clothes.

THE CHANGE FROM GAS LIGHT TO ELECTRIC LIGHT

I was about nine years old when we first experienced electricity in our homes. Electricity in our home was the greatest excitement of my life. We had an electric meter and we had to put in a shilling to turn on the electricity. A shilling was twelve cents. When the shilling was used up, the lights would go out leaving us in darkness. Suffice to say, we had to have a good stock of shillings on hand.

THE LAMPLIGHTER

There are so many things about which to write. I will try to give you, my reader, as much information as possible.

I remember when the lamplighter came around our street and lit the lamps about 4.30 p.m.

When the war began in 1939, there was no lighting of lamps.

I will write about the war years later.

FARMERS MARKET

We had a farmers market every Friday. The farmers

came to the city with fresh vegetables, chickens, etc. Everyone liked the market. It was an outing for all of us.

STREET VENDORS

The horse and cart was a great means for transportation. Men would sell fish from the cart. They came up the street shouting, "fish, fresh fish!" The people went to the cart and bought the fish. The fish were really fresh, "um." Another man sold vegetables and shouted out loud, "tatties, tatties, tatties!" Tatties are potatoes. The 'tattie' man came around every other day.

The milk was delivered to our door every day. It was in a glass bottle. The cream was on top so we had to shake the bottle to mix it well.

There was a lady who came to our door with a suitcase filled with all kinds of household items. I used to call her the kind lady. She always gave me a small gift like a handkerchief. Mother usually bought something from her.

WAR YEARS

At the beginning of the war, I remember putting on a play in the backyard, with my schoolmates, to raise money for the soldiers. We charged two cents for admission. We took the money that we received to the Mayor of Aberdeen.

When I look back over the years, I wonder how we ever made it. From eleven years old until I was seventeen, I only knew war. My life during those years wasn't a normal life for a child growing up. Surprisingly enough, we survived. We made the best of a bad situation.

One Autumn day when my family was listening to the radio while sitting near the fireplace, everyone became very serious. I didn't like the look on my Mother's face.

It was announced by the Prime Minister of England that Britain was at war with Germany. I was only eleven years old. I saw my Mother with tears in her eyes. All she said was, "Oh! my God, Oh! my God - it's happened!" I couldn't understand why she was so upset. What was this war thing anyway? Why was my Mother crying? I remember saying, "Don't cry Ma, I promise I will be good!" I was thinking, it was, maybe, my fault that the war started.

Funny isn't it that as children, we always blame ourselves for things that happen to our parents.

I was soon to learn that war was to affect everyone.

Our lives changed overnight.

The men enlisted in the armed forces.

My Father was in the Merchant Navy. My Brother joined the Royal Navy. He was an Officer. My Sister had a heart condition. She couldn't go and I was too young to be called up.

Life went on. School went on as before with quite a few exceptions.

Gas masks were given out to everyone. We had to carry them on our shoulder. If we forgot to take them to school, we were sent home to get them. An air raid shelter was put up in everyone's backyard. Sometimes, the air raid shelters were underground in the flats. We went to the underground shelters when the sirens went off. It was like a dugout underneath the building. There were wooden benches where we would sit until the 'all clear' sounded. Sometimes, we would be there for many hours.

I remember my Mother wakening me up in the middle of the night. "Get up, get up, hurry, hurry, no time to dilly dally." We all rushed down to the shelter. When the sirens went off in the middle of the night, we didn't have to go to school until 10 a. m.. Then, when we were in school, the sirens would go off again. There was no panic. We had to go to the shelter single file. There was no time for feeling sorry for ourselves. That was how it was. We had to obey the rules. We sang songs in the shelter and waited until the 'all clear' sounded. Then, we would go back to our classroom and resume our work.

I remember one evening, we were visiting my Mother's friend. She lived in a bungalow on Grampian Road, not too far away from our flat. The sirens went off, and we all went under the dining room table. We didn't make it to the shelter. There was a big explosion. The whole house shook. When the 'all clear' sounded, Ma and I went home. There was a big crater in the middle of the next street where we lived (Oscar Road). All of the windows in our home were blown out.

My Sister was standing in the lobby of our home with her boyfriend. He threw her to the floor and covered her so she wouldn't get glass all over her body. My Sister's heart problem caused her to be bedridden for over a year.

Another friend of mine was Betty Smith. We went to school together. She had a brother who was caught in the cross fire of a bomb. He died instantly. That was the first time in my life I saw someone in a coffin. I shall never forget that as long as I live.

Even to this day, it upsets me to see someone in a coffin.

My Mother had a friend, Mrs. Burnett, whose husband died at sea. The trawler he was on was never found. No one knows what happened. That is what I heard.

My Mother did a lot of work for the Church. She was always looking for donations. She was the secretary for the Ladies Work Party. When there were casualties, the Church hall served as a shelter. The ladies of the Work Party helped by making tea and sandwiches for the homeless until it was safe to return to their homes.

There was an army barracks at the Bay of Nigg. The soldiers guarded us during the rest of the war.

There would be Church dances for the servicemen stationed there and Mother made sure that everyone was looked after. Mother was quite the fundraiser, always helping others.

My childhood was never dull or lonely. There was always someone in our flat. The ministers would visit all the time. There were always cups of tea and, even though we were on rations, Mother seemed to have enough to share. It was like Jesus with the five loaves and two fishes. There always some left over!

Although we lived in a small flat, there was a time when Ma was asked if she could take in servicemen. How we managed, I will never know. I remember there were two airmen billeted with us. They slept in my Brother's bedroom. We managed fine. It is hard to imagine but this is all true.

The war made us very humble. We were all caring for each other. There was no time for snobbery. We were all in the same boat. We never worried about clothes but they were always clean. What we had, we looked after by pressing them. We always polished our shoes. They shone. We all took pride in our appearance.

The war lasted five years. I went from a child to a teenager. I met all different types of people. Mother cared for the soldiers by giving them meals. She said, "I hope people are good to your Brother, as well." He was in Greece during the war.

I remember a time when two soldiers who my friend, Phyllis and I had met, were invited into my Mother's home for a meal. After the meal, Phyllis and I and the two soldiers went to Phyllis' house for another meal. We were all filled up with the meal from my Mother. None of us was hungry. Phyllis' Mother was furious because she had gone to a lot of work cooking this lovely meal. She told us we had better eat the meal. Needless to say, we ate everything. This is another day, I shall never forget.

Well the war ended. We had become used to a different way of life. There were lots of heartaches. Some of the men didn't make it back. We were fortunate. My Brother came home safely and my Father came home safely. We resumed our new life.

The Canadian soldiers and American soldiers went back to their own countries. We will miss them because they played a big part in our lives.

CONCLUSION

This concludes my life from birth to a teenager.

I must say, I had a great childhood in spite of the war! The adoration I had for my Father and my Mother and the love I received from them while growing up as well as the experiences I gained during my childhood will never be forgotten. The love and experiences have inspired me to write this book. I had the best parents and the best friends. One cannot ask for more.

Love, in my estimation, is not love of money or possessions but love for each other from within the heart. I want to share the tears and joys that happened to me as a child until a teenager.

This concludes my memories from a child to a teenager.

Top Left - Jane Day, Dinah Day and 'Beauty', the dog

Bottom Left - Anthony Stanley Day (right) with friend - World War One - 1918

Top Right - Group picture - putting on play to raise money for the troops - Dinah in centre holding Red Cross can.

Bottom Right - Anthony Stanley Day (picture given to my mother, Jane, when they were courting)

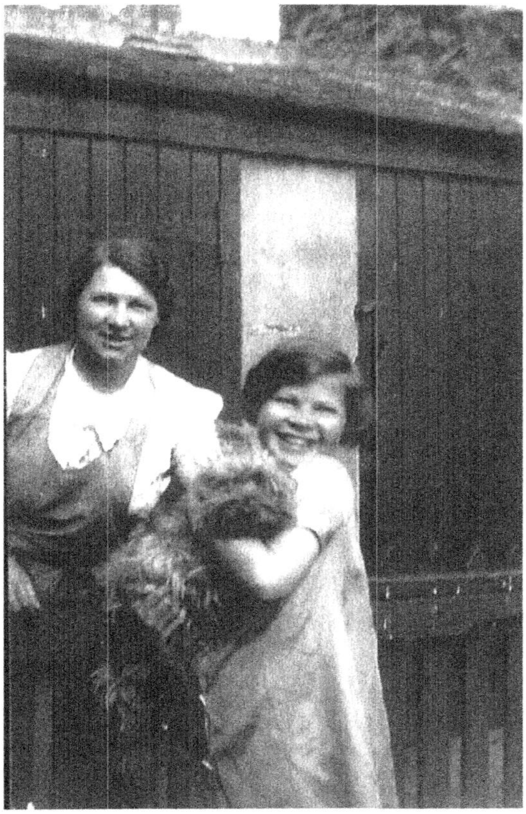

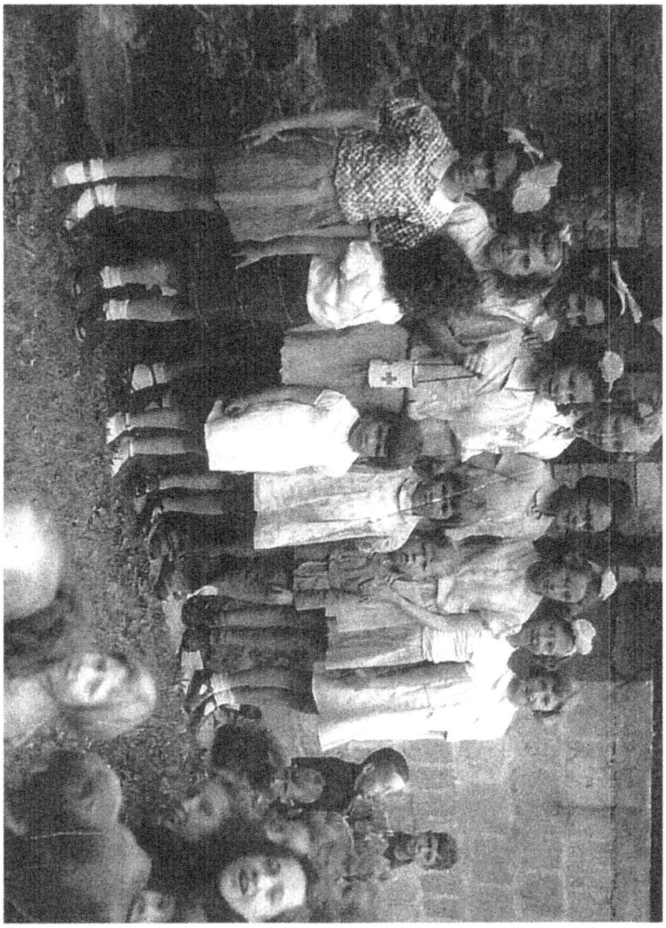

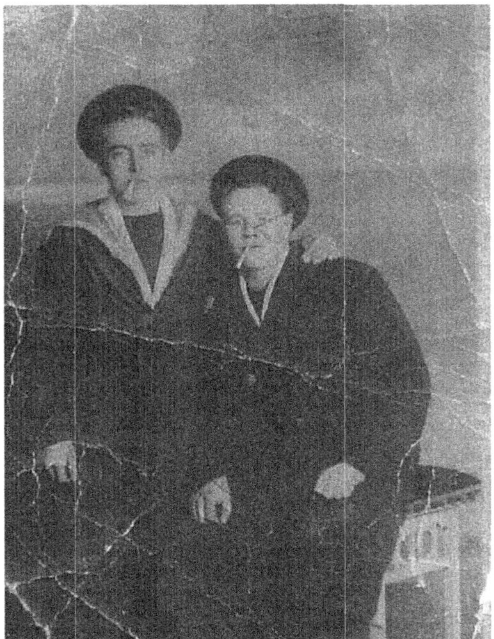

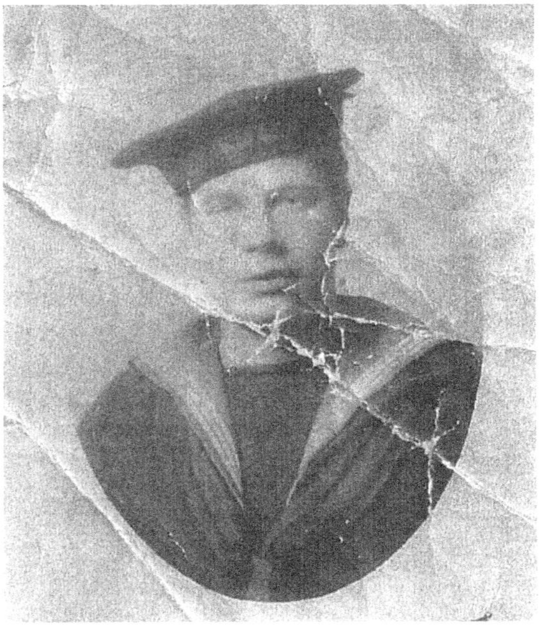

Top Left – Great Grandmother Reynolds (1850)

Top Centre – Grandmother Husband (nee Reynolds) (1872 - 1905)

Top Right – My mother, Jane Moody Husband – age 5

Bottom Left – Jane Husband, John Husband and Margaret Husband

War!

War!

This picture is of Sir Joshua Reynolds, a famous artist – 1723 to 1792. His paintings are in the Tate Museum in London, England.

This is as far back as I can go of the Family Tree.

War!

Top Left – Jane Day and Anthony Stanley Day – 1919

Bottom Left – Emma Reynolds Day (age 10)

Top Right – Stanley Day, Jane Day, Dinah Day, Anthony Stanley Day and Emma Reynolds Day (picture taken in backyard – 9 Glenbervie Road, Torry, Aberdeen, Scotland – 1944)

Bottom Right – Stanley Day – age 14

War!

Dinah Elizabeth Morrison (nee Day) - this picture was taken when I was age 50, London, Ontario. I am now 81 years old. I write short stories and poems. I decided to write a book about my childhood life. My children will pass this book on to their children and great-grandchildren.

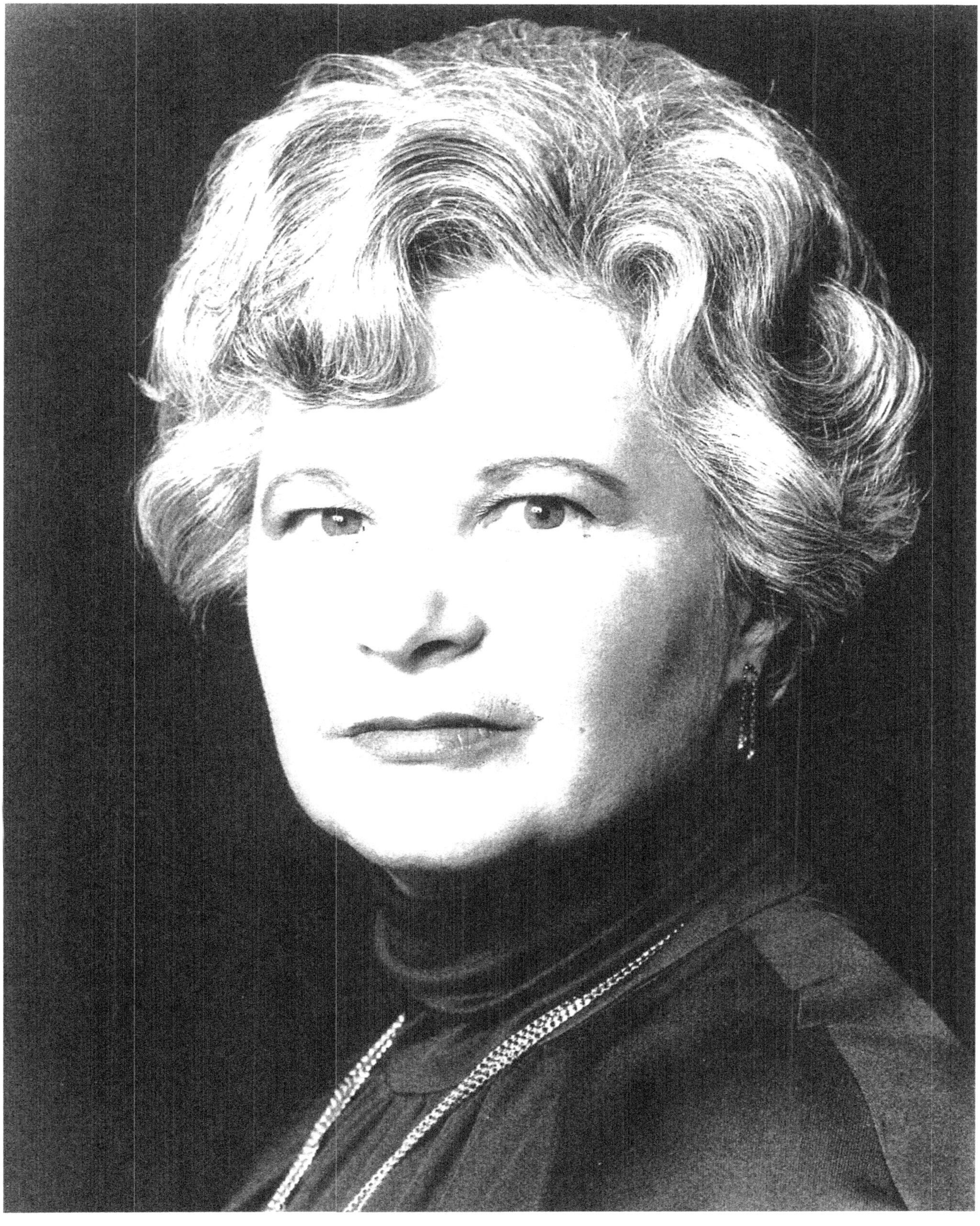

Printed in Great Britain
by Amazon